A Garden Full of Love

The Fragrance of Friendship

SANDRA KUCK

HARVEST HOUSE PUBLISHERS

Eugene, Oregon 97402

To My Friend

Trudee

With Love

Joupe

On

May Day 2000

J pushed the gate that swings so silently,

And I was in the garden and aware

Of early daylight on the flowers there

And cups of dew sun-kindled.

PAUL VERLAINE

Friendship is the
breathing rose,
with sweets in
every fold.

OLIVER WENDELL HOLMES

Friendship is the breathing rose · Friendship is the breathing rose · Friendship is the breathing rose · Friendship is the breat

Every act of kindness · Every act of kindness · Every act of kindness · Every act of kindness · Every act of kindness · Every act

Every act of kindness moves to a larger one till friendships
bloom to show what little deeds have done.

Awake, north wind, and come, south wind! Blow on my garden, that its fragrance may spread abroad.

THE SONG OF SONGS

*T*here has been rain in the night, and the whole garden seems to be singing—not the untiring birds only, but the vigorous plants, the happy grass and trees, the lilac bushes—oh, those lilac bushes! They are all out to-day, and the garden is drenched with the scent. I have brought in armfuls, the picking is such a delight, and every pot and bowl and tub in the house is filled with purple glory....

ELIZABETH AND HER GERMAN GARDEN

Every act of kindness · Every act of kindness · Every act of kindness · Every act of kindness · Every act of kindness · Every act of kindness · Every a

kindness

It is the simple things of life that make living worthwhile,

the sweet fundamental things such as love and duty,

work and rest, and living close to nature.

LAURA INGALLS WILDER

A friend may well be reckoned
the masterpiece of nature.

RALPH WALDO EMERSON

*The fragrance always remains
in the hand that gives the rose.*

HEDA BEJAR

The sweetest flower that blows,

I give you as we part.

For you it is a rose

For me it is my heart.

FREDERICK PETERSON

I wandered lonely as a cloud
That floats on high o'er vales and hills,
When all at once I saw a crowd,
A host, of golden daffodils,
Beside the lake, beneath the trees,
Fluttering and dancing in the breeze.

Continuous as the stars that shine
And twinkle on the milky way,
They stretched in never-ending line
Along the margin of a bay:
Ten thousand saw I at a glance,
Tossing their heads in sprightly dance.

I Wandered Lonely As A Cloud

The waves beside them danced; but they
Out-did the sparkling waves in glee;
A poet could not but be gay,
In such a jocund company;
I gazed—and gazed—but little thought
What wealth the show to me had brought:

For oft, when on my couch I lie
In vacant or in pensive mood,
They flash upon that inward eye
Which is the bliss of solitude;
And then my heart with pleasure fills,
And dances with the daffodils.

WILLIAM WORDSWORTH

What a pity flowers can utter no sound! —A singing rose,
a whispering violet, a murmuring honeysuckle,—oh,
what a rare and exquisite miracle would these be!

HENRY WARD BEECHER

Sandra Kuck

garden

They found so many wonders · They found so many wonders · They found so many wonders · They found so many wonders · They found

They ran from one part of the garden to another and found so many wonders that they were obliged to remind themselves that they must whisper or speak low. He showed her swelling leafbuds on rose branches which had seemed dead. He showed her ten thousand new green points pushing through the mould. They put their eager young noses close to the earth and sniffed its warmed springtime breathing; they dug and pulled and laughed low with rapture until Mistress Mary's hair was as tumbled as Dickon's and her cheeks were almost as poppy red as his.

FRANCES HODGSON BURNETT
The Secret Garden

A Rose

A sepal, petal, and a thorn

Upon a common summer's morn,

A flash of dew, a bee or two,

A breeze

A caper in the trees, —

And I'm a rose!

EMILY DICKINSON

They walked...and all along their way the wild June roses were blooming.
Laura gathered them until she filled Mary's arm with all she could hold.

"Oh, how sweet!" Mary kept saying. "I have missed the spring violets, but
nothing is sweeter than prairie roses. It is so good to be home again, Laura."

LAURA INGALLS WILDER
These Happy Golden Years

Every rose is an autograph from the hand of God on His world about us.

Arranging a bowl of flowers in the morning can give a sense of quiet in a crowded day—like writing a poem or saying a prayer.

ANNE MORROW
LINDBERGH

The Legend of the Forget-Me-Not

When to the flowers so beautiful
The Father gave a name,
There came a little blue-eyed one—
All timidly it came—
And standing at the Father's feet,
And gazing in His face,
It said with low and timid voice,
And yet with gentle grace,
"Dear Lord, the name thou gavest me,
Alas, I have forgot."
The Father kindly looked on him
And said, "Forget-me-not."

ANONYMOUS

"After all, the only real roses are the pink ones,"
said Anne, as she tied white ribbon around
Diana's bouquet ..."they are the flowers
of love and faith."

L. M. MONTGOMERY
Anne of the Island

"The whole earth is filled with his glory!" THE BOOK OF ISAIAH

Sandra Kuck

Full of His glory · Full of His glory · Full of His glory · Full of His glory · Full of His glory · Full of His glory · Full of His glory

The happy child rambled about, up and down hill. Nightingales sang, bees hummed, and butterflies flitted around him, and the most lovely flowers were blowing at his feet. He jumped about, he danced, he sang, and wandered from hedge to hedge and from flower to flower, with a soul as pure as the blue sky above him, and eyes that sparkled like a little brook bubbling from a rock. At last he had filled his basket quite full of the prettiest flowers; and, to crown all, he had made a wreath of field strawberry flowers, which he laid on the top of it, neatly arranged on some grass, and one might fancy them a string of pearls, they looked so pure and fresh.

THE FLOWER GATHERER
The Keepsake of Friendship

We have a little garden,
A garden of our own,
And every day we water there
The seed that we have sown,

We love our little garden,
And tend it with such care,
You will not find a faded leaf
Or blighted blossom there.

ANONYMOUS
Nursery Rhyme

blossom

ass · Every sort of grass · Every sort of grass · Every sort of grass · Every sort of grass · Every sort of grass · Every sort of grass

Then God said, "Let the land

burst forth with every sort of grass

and seed–bearing plant. And let

there be trees that grow seed–

bearing fruit. The seeds will then

produce the kinds of plants and

trees of like kind." And God saw

that it was good.

THE BOOK OF GENESIS

Let us be grateful to people who make

us happy; they are the charming

gardeners who make our souls blossom.

MARCEL PROUST

I do not think I have ever seen

anything more beautiful than the

bluebell I have been looking at. I

know the beauty of our Lord by it.

GERARD MANLEY HOPKINS

God's Expressions

Look without!
Behold the beauty of the day,
The shout
Of color to glad color,
Rocks and trees,
And sun and seas,
And wind and sky:
All these
Are God's expression,
Art work of His hand,
Which men must love
Ere they understand.

RICHARD HOVEY

Each little flower that opens, each little bird that sings—

He made their glowing colors, He made their tiny wings.

All things bright and beautiful, all creatures great and small,

All things wise and wonderful—the Lord God made them all.

CECIL F. ALEXANDER

beauty

y of the day · Behold the beauty of the day · Behold the beauty of the day · Behold the beauty of the day · Behold the beauty

Sandra Kuck ©1996

As spring came on, a new set of amusements became the fashion, and the lengthening days gave long afternoons for work and play of all sorts. The garden had to be put in order, and each sister had a quarter of the little plot to do what she liked with...for the girls' tastes differed as much as their characters. Meg's had roses and heliotrope, myrtle, and a little orange tree in it. Jo's bed was never alike two seasons, for she was always trying experiments; this year it was to be a plantation of sunflowers, the seeds of which cheerful and aspiring plant were to feed Aunt Cockletop and her family of chicks. Beth had old-fashioned, fragrant flowers in her garden—sweet peas and mignonette, larkspur, pinks, pansies, and southernwood, with chickweed for the bird and catnip for the pussies. Amy had a bower in hers—rather small and earwiggy, but very pretty to look at—with honeysuckles and morning-glories hanging their colored horns and bells in graceful wreaths all over it, tall white lilies, delicate ferns, and as many brilliant, picturesque plants as would consent to blossom there.

LOUISA MAY ALCOTT
Little Women

*A*s he was passing by...he saw a new girl in the garden—a lovely little blue-eyed creature with yellow hair plaited into two long tails, white summer frock, and embroidered pantalettes...Tom came up to the fence and leaned on it, grieving, and hoping she would tarry yet a while longer...But his face lit up, right away, for she tossed a pansy over the fence a moment before she disappeared.

MARK TWAIN
The Adventures of Tom Sawyer

My garden, with its silence and the pulses of fragrance that come and go on the airy undulations, affects me like sweet music. Care stops at the gates, and gazes at me wistfully through the bars. Among my flowers and trees, Nature takes me into her own hands and I breathe freely…

ALEXANDER SMITH

Perhaps the chiefest

attraction of a garden is

that occupation can always

be found there…with

mind and fingers busy, cares

are soon forgotten.

ALICIA AMHERST

I concluded that there is nothing better for people than to be happy and to enjoy themselves as long as they can. And people should . . . enjoy the fruits of their labor, for these are gifts from God.

THE BOOK OF ECCLESIASTES

*T*o analyze the charms of flowers is like dissecting music; it is one of those things which is far better to enjoy, than to attempt fully to understand.

HENRY THEODORE TUCKERMAN

How I love to be transported into a scented
Elizabethan garden with herb and Honey suckles,
and Roses clambering over a simple arbour...

ROSEMARY VEREY

But how great was his delight, on looking around him, to see

the fields spangled with flowers, as numerous as the stars of

heaven!—for the rain had nourished into blossoms thousands of

daisies, opened thousands of buds, and scattered pearly drops on

every leaf. Erick flitted about like a busy bee, and gathered away to

his heart's content.

THE FLOWER GATHERER
The Keepsake of Friendship

Friendship is precious · Friendship is precious · Friendship is precious · Friendship is precious · Friendship is precious · Friendshi

delight